DU

Words I Use

Around the House

Victoria Huseby

FRANKLIN WATTS
LONDON·SYDNEY

First published in 2005 by
Franklin Watts
96 Leonard Street
London
EC2A 4XD

Franklin Watts Australia
Level 17/207 Kent Street
Sydney, NSW 2000

Editor: Rachel Tonkin
Series design: Mo Choy
Art director: Jonathan Hair
Photography: Chris Fairclough
Literacy consultant: Gill Matthews

A CIP catalogue record for this book is
available from the British Library

ISBN: 0 7496 6087 2

Dewey classification: 643

Printed in China

Contents

About this book
This book helps children to learn key words in the context of when and where they are used. Each picture is described in the main text, and the words in bold are labelled on the picture along with other key words, as a starting point for discussion. The open-ended questions will also help with language development. On pages 22-23 a simple quiz encourages children to look again in detail at all the pictures in the book, and this can be used to develop referencing skills.

roof

What type of building do you live in?

farmhouse

cottage

terrace house

block of flats

4

Where you live

Where you live is your home. Some people live in a **house**, others live in a **flat**. There are large homes and small homes, homes in the country and homes in the town. Most homes have **doors**, **windows** and a **roof**.

bungalow

window

door

a housing estate

The living room

People relax in the living room. They may read the **newspaper** or listen to music on the **stereo**. Children often play with their **toys**.

What things do you do to relax?

plant

curtain

cushion

sofa

picture

newspaper

telephone

stereo

toys

table

photograph

picture

fireplace

television

videos

games

DVDs

8

lamp

mantlepiece

cushion

rug

armchair

By the fire

Some living rooms have a **fireplace**. In this room, you can sit in the **armchair** by the fire to watch **television**.

?

Where do you like to sit to watch television?

9

In the kitchen

You cook meals in the kitchen. Food is kept in **cupboards** or in the **fridge**. You bake or roast food in the **oven**. You use a frying pan or **saucepan** to cook on the **hob**.

?

What do you keep in the fridge in your kitchen?

fridge

bowl

mug

cupboard

kettle

toaster

saucepan

hob

oven

oven glove

egg box

11

At meal times

Sometimes you sit at a table for a meal. You use a **knife** and **fork** to eat your food.

glass

bread

knife

plate

fork

chair

water jug

Where else do you eat your food?

salad bowl

table cloth

serviette

beaker

iron

fruit bowl

tea towel

teapot

Using the sink

You use the **sink** to get water from the **tap**, wash up **dishes** or sometimes clothes. You use a **tea towel** to dry the dishes.

mirror

? What do you use when you get washed?

flannel

toothbrush

bath

tap

sponge

basin

In the bathroom

You clean your teeth and wash yourself in the bathroom. You use a **towel** to get dry after a **bath** or **shower**.

bubble bath

dressing gown

shower head

towel

In the bedroom

People sleep in a bedroom. Sometimes children play with **toys** here, too. Older children do their homework. People keep their clothes in a **chest of drawers** or cupboard.

pillow

bed

cuddly toys

slippers

duvet

cushion

In the garden

Some homes have a garden. **Flowers** and other plants may grow there. These children can play on the **grass** and on the **swing** and **slide**.

?

Where do you go to play outside?

climbing frame

wall

flowers

grass

trees

swing

slide

Can you spot . . . ?

A beaker on the table.

A chest of drawers.

A cuddly toy.

A cushion.

An egg box.

A flannel on the basin.

A kettle.

A photograph.

A plant behind the sofa.

A blue slide.

A red teapot.

A water jug.

Index